My President is Mean: 50 Rhymes On Cruel Choices And Why We Should Care

Text © 2025 Melvin   J. Coates Illustrations © 2025 Renegade Publishing.

This book is a work of political satire and commentary. While inspired by real events, it uses fictionalized language and characters to express protected opinion and parody under the First Amendment of the U.S. Constitution.

Printed in the United States of America First Edition, 2025

ISBN: 978-1-956088-10-6 (E-Book)

ISBN: 978-1-956088-08-3 (Paperback)

From the Author

My President is Mean! is more than a Teen to adult book — it's a bold call to awareness wrapped in rhyme.

I wrote it because I couldn't stay silent while Donald Trump's leadership — then and now — continues to harm real people. From slashing health and food programs to gutting global aid, his policies betray our nation's values of compassion and care.

Told through a child's voice, this book reveals serious truths: the powerful get the best science and care while denying it to those in need. That's not leadership — that's abuse of power.

Our kids are watching. They deserve better.

This book helps them see the difference between cruelty and courage, between selfishness and service. It's a tool to inspire a generation that leads with empathy, believes in truth, and lifts others up.

— Melvin J. Coates
Author, Veteran, and Believer in a Better America

Table of Contents

---***---

Climate Change References
Work Place Safety
Medicaid Cuts
Minimum Wage
Family Planning
Gun Control
Fair Housing
Police Reform
Education Cuts
Studen Loan Forgiveness
Disability Benefits   –
Universal Health Care
Environmental Research Cuts
Renewable Energy Cuts
Consumer Protection Enforcement
Equal Pay Opposition
Criminal Justice Reform
Cuts to Public Transportation
Food Safety Inspections

Arts Funding Cuts

DEI Cuts

Polliticization of the Census

Criminal Justice Reform

Environmental Justice initiatives

Public Preparedness

Affordable Housing

LGBTQ Opposition

 Cuts to Rural Development

Climate Change Mitigation

 Support for Public Broadcasting

My President is Mean

Family Separation Policy
Form: Ottava Rima

At borders where the desert winds do blow,

A cry rang out from tents in silent shame.

Small hands reached up, unsure of where to go—

A child alone, no face to match their name.

The law said "zero tolerance," and so

They split up families and played a cruel game.

A mother wept beneath the border sun,

While strangers claimed the damage must be done.

Muslim Travel Ban
Form: Limerick

From lands far away they had flown,
But found that the door wasn't shown.
"No Muslims!" they cried, As justice
denied— And hearts turned as heavy as
stone.

Ending DACA
Form: Limerick

A dreamer who studied all day
Was told they might soon go away.
"You're not really ours,"
Said voices with power—
Though they'd known just this country to stay

Title X Gag Rule
Form: Heroic Couplet

The doctors tried to help with all their might, But laws said silence was the thing most right. "Don't speak of choice," the rule came down like stone, And left the patients facing fear alone.

Transgender Military Ban
Form: Limerick

A soldier stood proud in their skin,
Yet some said, "You can't serve or win."
"We only want some,
The rest must succumb."
And prejudice marched right on in.

Withdrawal from Paris Climate Agreement
Form: Ottava Rima

The earth grew warm, the skies began to cry, But one great land just walked away in pride. While nations joined to cool the burning sky, This leader turned and took his country's side. "We'll drill and burn!" became the boldest lie, As icebergs cracked and ocean levels climbed. The world looked on with grief and great despair— A pact was signed, but missing someone there.

Rollback of Environmental Protections

Form: Ottava Rima

The rivers once so clean turned dark with grime,
The trees stood still as poison filled the air. A pen
was used to ruin nature's time, And profits grew
while animals grew rare. The skies grew thick with
soot, a silent crime, And gas replaced what once
was fresh and fair. All rules reversed, protections
torn apart— A victory for greed, a loss for heart.

Reduction of Refugee Admissions
Form: Heroic Couplet

The door once open wide began to close,
As weary feet were turned back from their woes.
"No room," they said, to families running scared,
While torch of hope flickered, cold and impaired.

Global Gag Rule Expansion
Form: Ottava Rima

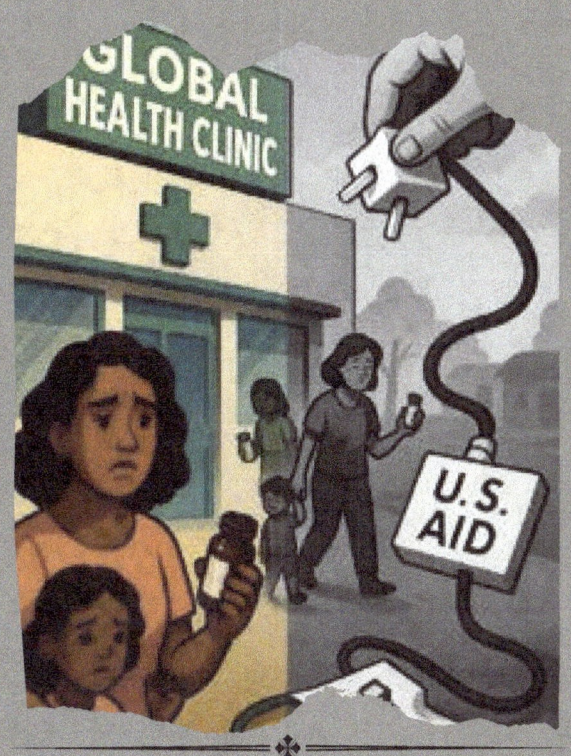

Across the globe, where care was hard to find,
Clinics closed their doors with heavy hearts.
For rules were changed by one with power blind,
Who silenced health and tore the world apart.
"No funds for you," the cruelest rule designed—
Unless you let the truth be torn from charts.
And so the help for women slipped away,
While health and hope began to fade each day

Cuts to SNAP Benefits
Form: Heroic Couplet

The kitchen shelves grew bare as nights grew long,
And hungry kids sang quiet hunger's song. The help
once offered vanished with a stroke— As wealth
grew fat, the poor were left to choke.

Attempted ACA Repeal
Form: Heroic Couplet

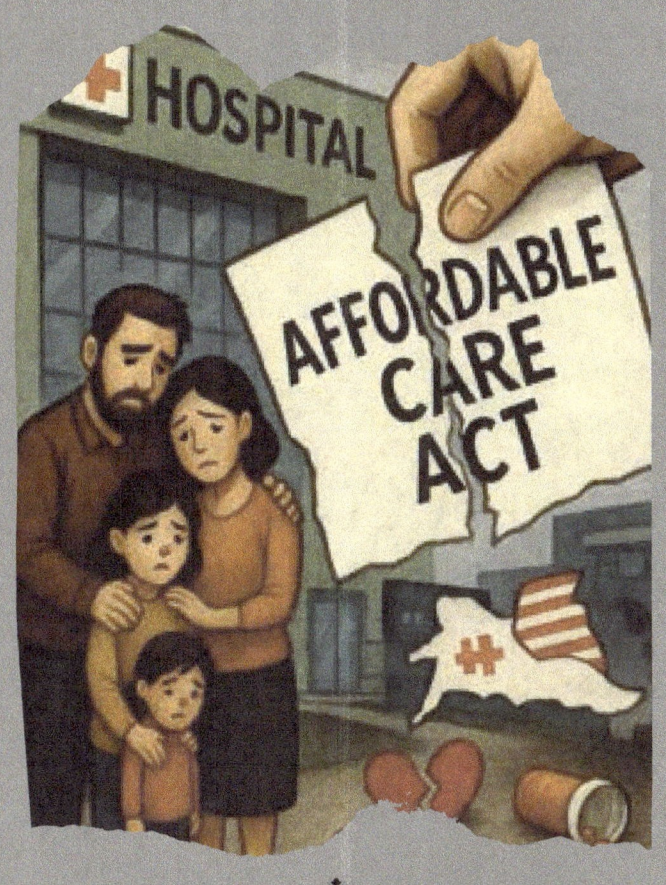

They promised care for every single soul,

Then took it back to chase a selfish goal.

With pens held high, they sought to take away

The hope that kept the doctor's bills at bay.

Opposition to Net Neutrality
Form: Limerick

The web was once open and free,
For folks just like you and like me.
But some made a fuss, Gave fast
lanes a plus— And left slower sites
lost at sea.

Pardoning Controversial Figures

Form: Heroic Couplet

With flourish, he forgave the ones condemned,

Though justice cried, he called them all his friends.

The guilty cheered while victims watched in pain—

A pardon signed, then pride without a shame.

Use of Emergency Powers
Form: Ottava Rima

A wall was built from bricks of fear and pride,
While laws were bent to make the money flow.
"Emergency!" the headline falsely cried— But
Congress sighed, for they had seen this show.
With funds re-routed, rules were pushed aside,
And what was fair was buried far below.
A leader claimed, "It's mine to take and choose,"
While checks and balances began to lose.

Attacks on the Press
Form: Heroic Couplet

"Fake news!" he'd shout with scowling,

Fiery glee, As truth grew dim and trust could barely be.

Reporters dodged the insults and the blame,

While facts and lies were treated just the same.

Undermining Voting by Mail
Form: Limerick

They warned us, "Your vote might get lost!"

Though facts showed that wasn't the cost.

With mailboxes gone,

And delays dragging on,

Our voices were silenced or tossed.

Revocation of TPS
Form: Heroic Couplet

They came to flee disaster, war, and fire—
But found new threats as promises expired.
A status once that kept them safe from fear
Was pulled away as justice failed to steer.

Restrictions on Asylum Seekers

Form: Ottava Rima

A door once open wide to those in need Was bolted shut with cruelty and might. "Go back," they said, "we will not hear your plead," As children wept alone throughout the night. The laws grew harsh, their hearts replaced with greed, And welcome mats were taken out of sight. A line of hope turned cold beneath the sun,
While justice, blind, ignored the pain begun.

Opposition to LGBTQ+ Rights
Form: Heroic Couplet

They stripped away the rights hard-earned with grace,
And told the youth, "You must now hide your face."
Where rainbows once had bloomed in open skies, They
passed new rules and whispered hurtful lies.

Elimination of Climate Change References
Form: Limerick

The climate, they claimed, was just fine,
Though fires and floods crossed the line.
With words they erased, From websites and space—
While Earth sent us sign after sign.

Reduction in Workplace Safety Regulations
Form: Heroic Couplet

The rules that kept the workers safe and sound
Were stripped away as profits gained new ground.
With fewer checks, more accidents arose—
But no one stopped the tide that only grows.

Cuts to Medicaid
Form: Ottava Rima

The sick and poor once found a helping hand, A path to care they couldn't reach alone. But those in power chose to take a stand Against the aid their own laws had once grown. They carved the budget, let the weak be banned, While wealth sat high upon a golden throne. The clinics closed, the nurses said goodbye— As health became a thing that cash could buy.

Opposition to Minimum Wage Increases
Form: Limerick

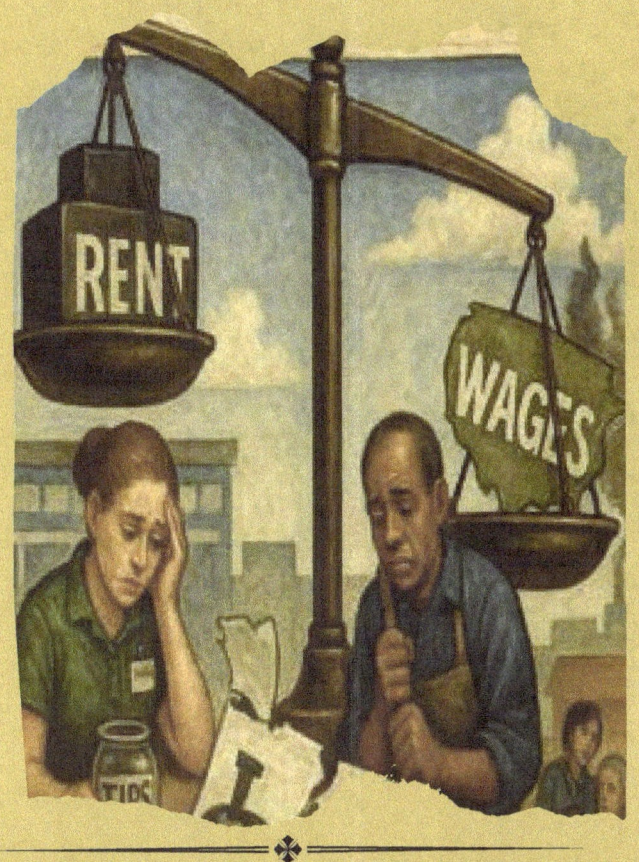

"A raise?" they said, "Not today."
Though folks worked hard every day.
With wallets so light,
They turned off the light—
And hoped they'd still find a way.

Family Planning Funding Restrictions

Form: Heroic Couplet

The clinics tried to help with care and grace, But funding vanished, leaving just a trace. Advice was hushed, the doctors made to fear— And choices blurred, no longer bright and clear

Opposition to Gun Control Measures
Form: Limerick

With shootings too many to name,
They still played the same old game.
"It's rights," they declared,
As kids sat and stared—
And no one was held to the blame.

Reduction in Fair Housing Enforcement
Form: Ottava Rima

The doors to homes once opened wide and bright Grew harder still for many to unlock. The rules that made things fair were dimmed from sight, While signs of "No Vacancy" seemed to mock. Discrimination hid in plain daylight, As hopeful renters faced another shock. And where there once was shelter, pride, and rest— Thhey found red lines and walls they must contest.

Opposition to Police Reform
Form: Ottava Rima

The people marched with signs held high and bold,
They chanted peace and begged the laws to bend.
But armored lines stood silent, Firm and cold,
Refusing change or promises to mend.
Though justice called, no answer did unfold,
Reform bills snapped, discarded in the end.
A dove took flight above the angry noise—
A hope for peace among the silenced voice.

27.

Cuts to Education Funding
Form: Heroic Couplet

The pencils broke, the books grew old and torn,
As dreams of kids were met with growing scorn.
The budget cuts took art and joy away— And left
dull walls where children used to play.

Opposition to Student Loan Forgiveness

Form: Ottava Rima

The cap and gown still shimmered in the light,
But burdens on their backs were heavy stone.
They climbed a hill that never reached its height,
For debts they bore, they battled all alone.
The dreams they chased were always out of sight—
A bill was torn while banks still held the throne.
Forgiveness came in whispers, not in laws,
As justice paused for politics to pause

Reduction in Disability Benefits
Form: Limerick

A boy in a chair looked around,
But help that he needed wasn't found.
The funds disappeared, And caregivers feared—
As silence replaced every sound.

Opposition to Universal Healthcare
Form: Heroic Couplet

"One plan for all" was shouted through the crowd,

But leaders turned away and said, "Not now."

While some paid more and others went without,

The promise of one care was filled with doubt.

Cuts to Environmental Research
Form: Limerick

They studied the earth and the sea,
To save what could vanish or flee.
But money was gone,
And science moved on—
While nature cried out, "Look at me!"

Opposition to Renewable Energy Initiatives

Form: Heroic Couplet

The windmills stopped, the solar panels cracked,

As coal grew rich and clean solutions lacked.

The sun still shined, but power turned to black—

And progress took a heavy step back.

Reduction in Consumer Protection Enforcement

Form: Ottava Rima

The rules once guarded every honest soul, From scams and cheats that prey on folks each day. But oversight grew smaller, lost control, While banks grew bold and led the game their way. The watchdogs turned and walked back to their hole, As wallets thinned and promises gave way. What once was fair now danced behind the scenes— A trick for profit, hidden in routines.

Opposition to Equal Pay Initiatives
Form: Heroic Couplet

Two workers stood with tools held in their hand,

But one earned less—though skills were just as grand.

"We work the same," she said, "yet paid unfair."

The boss just shrugged and looked the other way with flair.

Cuts to Mental Health Services

Form: Ottava Rima

The minds that hurt were left to drift alone, As clinics shut and phones would never ring. The help once there had vanished, overthrown, And silence grew where care should always cling. A voice cried out beneath a world unknown, While leaders claimed, "We cut another thing." But minds need light, not shadows dark and wide— For even brave hearts cry when hope's denied.

Opposition to Criminal Justice Reform
Form: Heroic Couplet

The jails were full of cries for second chance,

But mercy lost its place in law's advance.

The bars stayed shut though voices filled the air,

While justice slept in chains of cold despair.

Reduction in Public Transportation Funding

Form: Limerick

The buses grew rusty and slow,

While trains were too costly to go.

"We'll cut all the tracks,"

Said folks in big slacks—

While walkers got stuck in the snow.

Reduction in Food Safety Inspections

Form: Limerick

The food on the shelf looked quite fine,

But danger was hidden in brine.

With fewer checks made,

Some rules were delayed—

And sickness crept up down the line.

Cuts to Arts and Humanities Funding

Form: Heroic Couplet

❖

The paints dried out, the music lost its sound,

As classrooms watched the curtain hit the ground.

The arts once danced through every school and stage—

Now silenced by a budget's greedy cage.

Opposition to Anti-Discrimination Protections
Form: Heroic Couplet

The rules once stood to keep all people free,

But some erased them quietly, you see.

They claimed the laws were "too much, out of line"—

While fairness faded, one denied at a time

Politicization of the Census
Form: Limerick

❖

They counted, but not every head,

And some feared what questions had said.

"Will I be at risk?" Asked folks feeling brisk—

As justice and data both bled

Opposition to Environmental Justice Initiatives
Form: Heroic Couplet

---✦---

Where smoke poured thick in neighborhoods once green,
The cries for help were met with no machine.
While rich skies cleared, the poor breathed dirty air—
And leaders looked away, pretending fair.

Cuts to Public Health Preparedness
Form: Ottava Rima

The warnings came, but no one stocked the shelf,
The masks were gone, the plans were tossed away.
When illness struck, we had to fend ourselves—
No teams, no tools, just fear to lead the way.
What once was safe now trembled at each breath,
For cuts had carved the net that blocked out death.
And those who cried for help, they cried in vain—
As budgets slashed protection's strong domain.

Opposition to Paid Family Leave

Form: Limerick

A new mom returned in a week,
Though rest and support she did seek.
"We just can't delay," The boss had to say—
And tears rolled down her tired cheek.

Reduction in Affordable Housing Programs

Form: Heroic Couplet

The homes once planned were left as vacant lots,
While rents climbed high and safety came in spots.
The buildings rose, but only for the few—
The rest were told, "There's nothing here for you."

Opposition to LGBTQ+ Anti-Discrimination Measures
Form: Ottava Rima

The rainbow flag once blew above the door,
But now it's folded, faded by the rain.
The laws that kept all people safe and more—
Were tossed aside and labeled as a strain.
"Just be yourself" now whispered like a chore,
As teachers taught but dared not to explain.
And those who once stood proud began to hide—
For safety, not for shame, they stepped aside

Cuts to Rural Development Programs
Form: Limerick

The roads turned to dust with no plan,
And broadband just wouldn't run.
They promised and left,
As farms faced the theft—
Of help that had barely begun.

Opposition to Climate Change Mitigation Efforts

Form: Heroic Couplet

The oceans rose while leaders raised their hand—
Not to fix, but to delay what's planned. The
glaciers cried, the forests choked with flame, Yet
profit always seemed to win the game.

Reduction in Support for Public Broadcasting
Form: Limerick

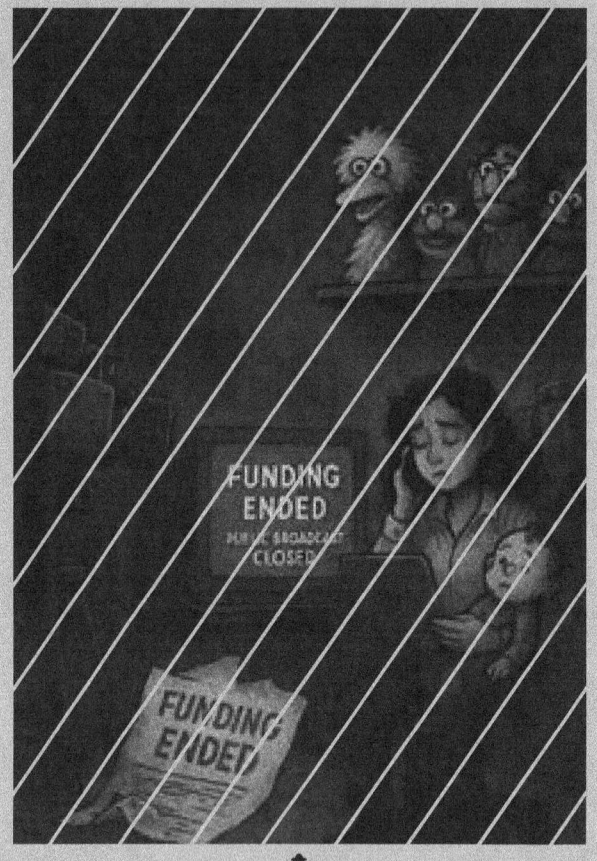

The channel went dark overnight,
No stories, no shows left in sight.
"No room in the plan,
" Said one suited man—
"For learning or laughter or light."

My President is Mean

References

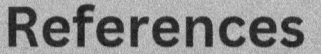

1.Immigration & Refugees
American Civil Liberties Union. (2018). Family separation by the Trump administration. https://www.aclu.org
National Immigration Law Center. (2020). DACA and TPS updates. https://www.nilc.org
2.Healthcare & Social Services
Kaiser Family Foundation. (2020). Title X and Gag Rule. https://www.kff.org
Center on Budget and Policy Priorities. (2020). SNAP, Medicaid, and poverty programs. https://www.cbpp.org
3.Climate & Environment

U.S. Environmental Protection Agency. (2017-2020). Environmental deregulation under Trump. https://www.epa.gov
National Resources Defense Council. (2019). Paris Agreement and Trump withdrawal. https://www.nrdc.org
4.Civil Rights & LGBTQ
Human Rights Campaign. (2020). Trump's rollback of LGBTQ+ protections. https://www.hrc.org

Lambda Legal. (2020). Military ban and transgender rights. https://www.lambdalegal.org 5.Education & Student Loans U.S. Department of Education. (2020). Cuts to public education and student loan forgiveness. https://www.ed.gov 6.Technology & Communications Federal Communications Commission. (2018). Net neutrality rollback. https://www.fcc.gov 7.Housing, Labor, and Economy U.S. Department of Housing and Urban Development. (2019). Fair housing enforcement rollback. https://www.hud.gov Economic Policy Institute. (2018). Opposition to minimum wage increases and equal pay. https://www.epi.org

8.Public Health
Centers for Disease Control and Prevention. (2020). Pandemic preparedness and response under Trump. https://www.cdc.gov
World Health Organization. (2020). Impact of global gag rule expansion. https://www.who.int

9.Criminal Justice & Policing
The Sentencing Project. (2020). Trump-era resistance to criminal justice reform. https://www.sentencingproject.org
10.Media & Censorship
Committee to Protect Journalists. (2019). Attacks on the press and freedom of speech. https://cpj.org
11.General Government Actions
Congressional Research Service. (2020). Emergency declarations and executive power under Trump. https://crsreports.congress.gov
Brennan Center for Justice. (2020). Voting suppression and politicization of the census. https://www.brennancenter.org

EXPLORE THE WORLD OF

PUBLISHER : RENE

Discover Engaging Stories

LOS DOS PAPAS DE YESICA

AUTOR:
MELVIN J. COATES

ILUSTRADOR:
JAVIER HEREDIA

My First Trace Book
ABCs and 123s

ABC

12345
67890

A

Melvin J Coates and Carlitta C. Coates

Jessica's
Two Dads

By Melvin J. Coates
Illustrated By: Scribbleline

books.melvincoates.com

...AVE A REVIEW
...ACK MATTERS

www.ingramcontent.com/pod-product-compliance
Lightning Source LLC
Chambersburg PA
CBHW070942120626
46546CB00004B/1528